Uncle Frank 'Sez'

Published by CelebrityPress™, Orlando, FL
A division of The Celebrity Branding Agency®

Celebrity Branding® is a registered trademark
Printed in the United States of America.

LCCN: 2011923893
ISBN: 9780982908396

This publication is designed to provide accurate and authoritative information with regard to the subject matter covered. It is sold with the understanding that the publisher is not engaged in rendering legal, accounting, or other professional advice. If legal advice or other expert assistance is required, the services of a competent professional should be sought. The opinions expressed by the authors in this book are not endorsed by CelebrityPress™ and are the sole responsibility of the author rendering the opinion.

Most CelebrityPress™ titles are available at special quantity discounts for bulk purchases for sales promotions, premiums, fundraising, and educational use. Special versions or book excerpts can also be created to fit specific needs.

For more information, please write:

CelebrityPress™,
520 N. Orlando Ave, #44,
Winter Park, FL 32789

or call 1.877.261.4930

Visit us online at www.CelebrityPressPublishing.com

Uncle Frank 'Sez'

LIFE LESSONS FROM THE FRONT PORCH OF A SELF-MADE MAN!

by Tracy Myers, CMD

......featuring Beth Chapman

A book of 'Frankisms' that we should all remember

Acknowledgement

Writing a page of "Thank You's" is a MUCH more intimidating and daunting task than writing a book. If people don't like the book, it's their prerogative. If you forget to thank someone that thinks they deserve to be thanked, you're deleted from their Facebook friends list. With that being said, and against my better judgement, here are the folks I'd like to thank.

My Lord & Savior Jesus Christ, my wonderful mom for always believing in me, my loving & supportive wife for being my rock and my best friend, my incredible kids for keeping me young at heart, my grandparents for creating a legacy of integrity for me to pass along to my children, Michael York for being my mentor and inspiring me on my journey of becoming uncommon, Beth Chapman for writing such an inspiring forward for this book, my Frank Myers Auto Maxx team members for being the best Automotive Solutions Providers in the industry and for "minding the store" while I check some other things off of my bucket list, for my friends Eric & Candy Seagraves for sharing a lifetime of memories with me...may there be many more to come, Bruce Roffey for being my friend & business partner PLUS for choosing me as his mentor (little does he know that he mentors me as much as I do him), my marketing mentors Jimmy Vee & Travis Miller for helping me take my marketing efforts from good to great, the folks at Celebrity Press for helping me turn this book into a reality and our Pastors at Agape Faith Church for preaching the uncompromising word of God.

Finally, it would be a travesty if I didn't thank my dad…the one and only Uncle Frank. He was not only the inspiration for this book but he's played a huge part of my success in life and in business. "Thank You" is not enough for all you've done for me. I love you, appreciate your guidance and hope you think this book does justice to our families' legacy.

Contents

Introduction
By Beth Chapman

We all have special people who have had an overwhelming influence on us throughout the years. They are supportive, inspiring and encouraging. Often times they are mentors or heroes, and impact who we are in such a profound way that they become larger than life to us, and we strive to be just like them. Such is the case with Tracy Myers and Uncle Frank.

When Tracy Myers first contacted me, he said he was writing a book about his beloved Uncle Frank and his many "sayings," which he referred to as Uncle "Frankisms." While some people might find that strange, being from the south, having had a "Big Mama" and an Uncle Homer who owned a country store, I knew exactly what he meant.

"Isms" are those little nuggets of wit and wisdom passed

down from generation to generation each in its own unique language. They have stood the test of time. They are common sense approaches to business and to life that if followed, can motivate and inspire you to become your best in every endeavor.

Tracy learned from Uncle Frank, like all of us learn from our relatives, things that are not taught elsewhere. They are homegrown statements that say 'a whole lot with a very little.' They have been obtained through life lessons and personal experiences that cannot be learned in any classroom of a business school, only in the classroom of life.

I soon discovered that Uncle Frank and the powerful impact he has had on Tracy's life is more than a story, it is feeling – a very deep feeling of pride and accomplishment, of love and respect. It is the very foundation on which Tracy has lived his life and built his business and his reputation. Tracy shared with me that Uncle Frank was a combination of his dad and all that he had taught him, combined with the influences of Zig Ziglar, John Wayne and many more successful businessmen. This truly made Uncle Frank more than merely a good man or a smart man. It made him a larger than life character in the eyes of Tracy Myers.

If what Tracy described to me could be painted, it would be the quintessential Norman Rockwell painting – a down-to-earth portrait of business and of life.

I quickly realized through corresponding with Tracy that this book would be a legacy project for him - a love letter of appreciation to his father for all that he had taught him and a written legacy for which he wanted his children, friends and employees to aspire. It was to be an instruction book on the lessons of life and business for anyone who dared to read them, much less follow and take them to heart.

Tracy Myers' desire to share with the world what Uncle Frank taught him is a personal mission of how using this knowledge has made him the man he is today both personally and professionally. In his quest to share all that he has learned from Uncle Frank, he has celebrated his legacy of love and learning and the success he has acquired from it. In doing so, he has created a how-to-book of life and business for anyone who dares to read it, much less take it to heart and practice it.

To have received the Uncle "Frankisms" is one thing, but to pass them on to his children, his employees and now the world, is a gesture of kindness. Once you read them you will forever be grateful. While Tracy uses this book to show appreciation of Uncle Frank's influence on his life and how it has made him the person he is today, don't let his humility fool you. There is little difference in what Uncle Frank taught and what Tracy learned to use.

Tracy is a successful businessman and in my professional opinion, a marketing genius. There is no doubt that he has taken everything Uncle Frank taught him and used it for good – the good of his family, his associates, his business and his customers. Uncle "Frankisms" are more than quotable quotes; they are meaningful words and valuable lessons from which we can all learn.

What Uncle Frank gave Tracy Myers was the foundation on

which he has built and become a successful entrepreneur, a marketing visionary, a best selling author and the owner of an automobile empire that started with the first Frank Myers store more than 83 years ago. This definition is not one of a financial statement, though it could be – it is a statement about his genuine care and concern for his customers and seeing to it that they are treated with respect – much like family, just like Uncle Frank taught him.

This book is filled with words of wisdom and wit that have been tested, tried and proven to be beneficial in leading anyone who takes them to heart to levels of greater personal and professional growth.

Read this book and you are guaranteed to learn, laugh, live and love a little more each and every day – as you come to know the wit and wisdom of Uncle Frank and the overall success it can bring you.

- Beth Chapman is the author of four books including the national award-winner, "The Power of Patriotism . . . The Speech **Heard** *Around the World." Her latest book is "If God Makes Spiritual Fruit, Then Why Am I a Nut? Discover why life is a comedy and not a tragedy." For more information on her please visit www.bethchapman.com.*

Foreword

So Who Is Uncle Frank?

Uncle Frank is a great man. He is as wise as he is old. He has a southern charm about him that makes him a gentleman's gentleman and a man of honor. He has more business savvy on his worst day than any high falootin' Wall Street lawyer has on his very best day. He operates with only two words in his business vocabulary: honesty and integrity. He doesn't know doing business any other way. You'd better hope you don't either or he'll sure call you out on it.

Like most brilliant entrepreneurs, he is crazy – 'crazy like a fox', that is. Uncle Frank is so smart that his mind never stops working. Because of that his thoughts don't either, so sometimes they get to his mouth before they've been fully processed by his brain. Translated, that means that he is

15

brutally honest. He says all the things most people think, but don't have the courage or ability to say. When it comes to being politically correct, Uncle Frank just ain't your kinda guy. Thank goodness! That's what makes him so unique in today's politically correct "yes man" world.

He is an All-American guy. He is red, white and blue to the core and no one is more proud to be an American than he is. He loves God, his family and his country. He appreciates the men and women of the United States Military, and I've even seen his eyes well up with tears as he's heard the *Star Spangled Banner* at a ball game as he takes his hat off and places his hand over his heart.

Uncle Frank believes in democracy, a free-market economy and capitalism at its best. He is a staunch conservative in his business principles as well as his personal ideals. He believes in getting more with less and making customers more than just customers – they are his friends. Uncle Frank doesn't just talk about family values – he lives them.

There has never been a man, short of the Lord Jesus Christ, who has loved me more or taught me more about business and about life than Uncle Frank. I think you will find his pearls of wit and wisdom to be not only true, but most helpful if you will just apply them to your daily life. Reading them is easy, applying them takes effort.

Uncle Frank is solid, as hard as a rock. He's worked for everything he's ever gotten and he expects everyone else to do the same. He doesn't mind helping people who can't help themselves, but he's not for helping anyone who can help themselves but won't.

Uncle Frank can be like a huge grizzly bear if you mess with his God, family, country or customers, but deep down inside, he is a big lovable teddy bear – one who might even shed a tear every now and then.

He is the epitome of John Wayne, Will Rogers, Lee Iacocca, Charlton Heston, Sam Walton, Jerry Clower and Zig Ziglar all rolled into one, but he is no man's fool – not for one minute. You just cross him and you will find out.

He's also a little like a southern gentleman's version of Donald Trump in that he's street-smart, has business savvy, knows what he wants and goes after it full speed ahead. He doesn't make excuses and he lets nothing get in his way of doing what he thinks is right.

Uncle Frank is a little bit of everything and a whole lot of something – something special and unique, that is – a dying breed of American men that just don't exist in today's business world again. They just don't make men like that anymore – those who say what they mean and mean what they say. When he makes a business deal with you and shakes hands on it, you can take it to the bank. His word is his bond and it's as strong as any 100-year-old oak you can find.

When Uncle Frank considers you a friend, he is your friend in good times and in bad times. As a matter of fact, he may even grow closer to you in the bad times because he knows that's when you need him the most.

He believes in making a good living, but believes he can make money without robbing you of yours. He will give you the best deal he's got. He genuinely wants you both to be happy with your business transaction at the end of the day.

Uncle Frank loves wheelin' and dealin' in and of itself. The profit never really matters to him. Sometimes he is even willing to take a loss. He just loves the 'chase' – the 'sell'. It doesn't even matter what he's selling as long as he's selling. He loves it that much. So much in fact, that he'd just as soon trade for a mule as a Rolex.

It is my hope that as you read along in this book, you will take in all the Uncle "Frank-isms" you can, so that you can benefit from his years of experience and knowledge too. I don't want to be selfish and keep him all to myself; I want to share him with the world.

Why would I want you to beat your head against a wall all day long trying to figure out the meaning of life, how to motivate your employees, treat your customers or increase your sales when I can simply tell you what Uncle Frank has taught me all these years? It will save you lots of energy and effort.

Just read along and if you learn just one half of all that I have learned from what Uncle Frank 'sez', you'll be feelin' mighty fine and on your way to greater successes now and in the future than at any other time in your life.

Uncle Frank is "John Wayne, Will Rogers, Lee Iacocca, Charlton Heston, Sam Walton, Jerry Clower and Zig Ziglar all mixed into one..."

Frankism #1

"You can't lead others unless you have followed."

Uncle Frank is always quick to point out that no member of the Boy Scouts has ever started out as an Eagle Scout and no member of the United States Military has ever started out as a general. They have to work their way up through the ranks and into those positions of leadership. They have to earn those titles through dedication and hard work.

They can only accomplish those positions once they have perfected the skill, endurance and perseverance it takes to follow. They have to spend time in the trenches – training, learning and perfecting multiple tasks before they can reach that rightful role of leadership.

There is a right of passage they must endure in order to achieve that caliber of leadership. They must 'serve their time in the vineyard.' They must follow and become good followers in order to become great leaders.

Patton, MacArthur and Schwarzkopf sure did. Then there were great men like Audie Murphy, who were great followers who led so well that they earned the highest decorations attainable, though they were not the highest-ranking leaders in their field.

We are all the same, no matter what profession we are in – we have to follow first before we can lead. Shadowing someone else who has been in the business or being mentored by an expert in the field is highly recommended in any occupation.

Just as we have to crawl before we can walk, and walk before we can run, we must also learn before we can teach, and follow before we can lead.

Being a follower means learning, being trained and drawing knowledge from someone else and their experience. Why would any person turn down good advice based on prior experience? No smart person would. By following, you learn the ropes and see the possible pitfalls, and you can learn to dodge them instead of plummeting headlong into them.

There are many land mines in the business field, so it is best to follow someone who knows where they are. Then, when it's your turn to cross the field by yourself, you'll know where each land mine is buried and you can avoid them. It will save your life.

Be patient in learning to follow and you will be great in learning to lead. We have to do one before we can do the other. Follow the leader, and then you can lead the followers.

Frankism #2

"To achieve maximum success, customers must love your process as much as your products."

The perfect example of this Uncle Frankism is McDonald's. No matter where you are, Russia, China or any of our 50 states, you can go to a McDonald's and get basically the same hamburger. Their company's processes are solid, tested and proven to be effective. That is one of the reasons they have achieved maximum success.

Most famous for their fries, they have the same fries in all of their international locations. They have taken ordinary potatoes (which anyone can buy) and created a product that millions of people around the world love.

Whether its Poland or Alaska, McDonald's fries are cooked

the same way, in the same type of fryer, with the same type of oil, and the same amount of salt added. They taste the same and are served fresh and hot (in basically the same types of paper bags and boxes).

They have perfected not only their product, but also their process – what they purchase, how they preserve its flavor and how they cook, wrap and present it.

People want their food fast and consistent. McDonald's gives them that.

There may be a different or better burger down the street, but if people see a McDonald's while on a trip, they know what they will get – the same fast food packaged in the same way they get it at home. People know that McDonald's processes are as good and reliable as their products.

When Uncle Frank was looking for a way to grow his car dealership, he turned to McDonalds for inspiration. He knew he would have to create a process that customers loved, and required that it be customer-friendly. In order to provide such, Uncle Frank eliminated commission-based sales in an effort to remove an outdated, unfriendly process.

He wanted his customers to have a better car shopping experience, instead of being hassled by a salesperson whose next paycheck depended on how much over invoice price they could charge their customers. So, he developed a consistent customer-friendly process of selling cars.

It became a well-known fact that buying a car from Uncle

Frank was an easy and pleasant process – honesty, fairness, prices posted right on the car, and all the free information that a car shopper wanted, with NO pressure to buy <u>today</u> and a quick and friendly check-out process, but not a hectic all day affair.

The process of buying a car at Uncle Frank's became as good as the cars he sold. As a result, he sold more of them.

Frankism #3

"If someone else can make it better, faster and less expensive than you can, then what can you do differently?"

It seems like there are millions of car dealerships. Most all of them look alike. They are cookie cutter shiny, well-lit show rooms with cars, cars and more cars. There is usually a guy wearing a suit 'stalking' you and your family, lurking behind cars, then approaching you asking questions in an attempt to find out how much money you have.

Early in the game, a light bulb went off in Uncle Frank's head, which it did on a regular basis. It dawned on him that all the car dealerships buy the same cars from the same places, pay the same thing for them and they all look just alike. If everything was the same, what could he do to set himself apart, to stand out from the others? He wanted to be "different" – unique, noticeable and memorable.

So he put on his supersonic thinking cap (as only he could do), and soon became all those things and more. He opened a gourmet coffee bar in his car dealership and provided a free *new school* arcade for the kids complete with an X-Box plus an *old school* arcade for the young-at-heart adults complete with a Ms. Pac Man and Donkey Kong. He also added Flat Screen televisions featuring a FREE Family Movie Night, popcorn included – for everyone whether they bought a car from him or not.

If you think that's the cake, then those who did buy cars from him could have their cake and eat it too – with an iron-clad money back guarantee and warranty for the lifetime of their car.

It's no secret that Uncle Frank's prices were competitive. His goal was not to be the "cheapest," but the best. What he includes is honest, dependable and different in many ways – in an effort to meet all of your needs and more.

There are as many different types of business people as there are businesses. They all have their own way of accomplishing their goals and striving to be successful. As for me though, I just prefer Uncle Frank's way because I believe it's the best way – (not that I'm biased or anything).

Frankism #4

"If you don't know what makes your brand great you can't expect anyone else to."

In the business world, believe it or not, it is not always about being the best, but it's about having the best sales environment and the best atmosphere for your business.

The one thing potential car buyers don't like is feeling the pressure of knowing that car salesmen get a huge commission on their 'sell'. Once again, Uncle Frank saw and felt what the customer wanted and he gave it to them. He came up with something different than most car dealerships – a safe and comfortable place to shop, free from being hassled into a deal you don't want, based on an over-zealous salesman's need for a commission.

Uncle Frank decided to provide non-commissioned sales professionals with a regular salary and bonuses for going above and beyond the call of duty and exceeding the customer's expectations. In other words, they got paid, but it wasn't based on how much money they could make on a customer's deal.

Since the number one thing potential buyers hate is the commissioned salesman who focuses on nothing other than their money, Uncle Frank changed the entire culture of the car sales business. It transcended the experience for the customer and allowed them to take their minds off their wallets and focus on the best car for them and their family.

It produced an honest environment, where a young man in his thirties looking for a family car for his wife and four children, didn't walk out with a signed contract and new keys for a Porsche 911.

It also ensured that the sales professionals were focused more on being honest and making the customer happy than receiving a commission so they could take their family to Hawaii. This new culture was much more conducive to a win-win situation, so that both the customer and the sales professionals appreciated and benefited from it immensely.

Frankism #5

"Your employees cannot outsource the passion needed to excel in today's marketplace."

Passion can be seen, felt and heard. It has to be so deeply rooted in your spirit that you cannot hide it. It has to be obvious in everything you do – the way you sound with your voice, smile with your eyes and the way you say, "Hello, may I help you?" Passion has to be seen in the way you walk and the way you talk. It has to be genuine - if it's not, the customer or any other person you are dealing with will know it.

Nobody likes a "fake", and most people can see one from a mile away – so be genuine or don't be at all. Some people are so fake being "fakey" that they can't even fake being "fakey."

People want "real" people to wait on them, to show them the solution they want and need. They want a pleasant experience. They want to leave your place of business happy. It's your job to make sure they leave even happier than when they came in. If they do, they'll come back again and again. That's what passion will get you.

You can't show what you don't have, so if you don't have passion, then get it quickly. *If you love what you do, you will always do what you love.*

Find your passion, show your passion, live your passion and share that passion with others, and you'll always be good at what you are passionate about doing.

Frankism #6

"Your customer will pay almost anything if you give them an experience they will remember."

This quote from Uncle Frank begs the question once again: "Why will a customer pay $4 for a Starbuck's coffee when they can get one for 50 cents at a local gas station? Better yet, why would they pay $5 more for a 3D movie, when they can't even keep the glasses?

It is all about the "experience" that you give them that no one else can – even when you're offering the same product.

So what if the paying customer wants to keep the glasses as a reminder of their first date or their first 3D movie? Let 'em. It goes back to "selling" them the way they want to be sold to keep them coming back for more.

35

The same product with the same price will sell better if they are given an experience by one, that they may not be afforded by the other.

Be the one that gives a little more, the one that is different and more considerate of the customer. Give them an "experience" they won't forget.

Frankism #7

"Be significant in your customers lives. Make them feel good."

Most people remember their first bicycle, their first car, computer, their first prom dress and the list goes on and on. They also remember how they felt and where they were the day Elvis Presley died, Kennedy was shot or when the World Trade Center was bombed.

People remember their "experiences" and how they felt then and how they feel in all situations.

That is why your customers have to do more than just purchase something at your place of business. He or she needs to feel good about you and the way that you do business.

They are going to have an "experience" in your place of business. It will be a good experience, a bad experience or an indifferent one. One way or other, they will have one. And the people with the good experiences will come back again!

Make your customers feel special and become a part of their lives. If you sell electronics, then be the person they go to when they need electronics. Be the person they refer their friends to as well.

The American poet, Maya Angelou wrote:

"I've learned that people will forget what you said, people will forget what you did, but people will never forget how you made them feel."

People pay not only for the products you sell, but for the way you "sell" them, the way you treat them and yes, the way you make them feel. They deserve the best experience possible so give them one. They'll be glad you did and you will too when you see them come back for years to come.

Frankism #8

"Take time to share what you know with someone who wants to be where you are."

Years ago when someone took a young, inexperienced person under their wing to train them, they called it an apprenticeship. Today, they call it mentoring. Whatever you choose to call it – it is a good thing according to Uncle Frank. I know because I have become the man I am today because of Uncle Frank and his wisdom, wit and knowledge.

What makes Uncle Frank such a unique and well-loved man is not only that he is so generous, kind and good, but because he wants to share his pearls of wisdom with other people. He wants to "give back" and he has through me and so many other people. Uncle Frank used to "pay it forward," before it became a popular saying.

Another concept that Uncle Frank mastered long before it became a household phrase was "tough love." He knew how and when to push a person to take the extra step they needed to take. He knew just how to make someone fend for themselves and work for what they got. He knew how to "let go" and force someone to learn a lesson - sometimes the hard way. He knew if they did, they would never forget it. It would be with them forever.

It is never enough to grow and develop on our own. The prize comes when we pass our knowledge along to other people in an effort to give back and be thankful to God for all the blessings he has given us. Uncle Frank continues to share with me and so many others and helps us grow in wisdom and knowledge.

As a result, I am more willing to give to others and help them grow because of it. You should be too. Don't keep all your talents, skills and abilities to yourself. Share them with other people and you will be rewarded in many ways.

People want to be where you are, so help them get there. After all, good people surround themselves with other good people. You can gain a whole lot more in togetherness than being all alone.

Frankism #9

"You can't save your way to a profit because nuthin' from nuthin' is still nuthin'."

A professional comedian once said of the Wendy's Hamburger's 99 cent special, "A 99 cent special ain't no special if you ain't got 99 cents."

Another old saying is that 80% of something is better than 100% of nothing.

To be prosperous in business for very long you have to make a profit. Sure you can save and save, cut corners and be conservative in your spending, but that won't make you a profit.

You have to turn a profit and make an income. That translates

41

into selling your products or services to people. It also means getting creative and coming up with new ways to make money. Perhaps you'll give away an inexpensive gift totally free just to get people in the store to shop – hoping they'll buy something while they're there. There are all sorts of legitimate gimmicks to get customer's attention, but the bottom line is that you have to sell them.

Uncle Frank 'sez', "You can't spend what you don't have, you shouldn't buy what you don't need and you should take care of what you own." While that is great advice, he knows and you and I do too, that we have to sell something to get something – a profit. Without it, we can't keep our doors open very long.

Don't focus on saving as much as you do selling. Don't focus on outcome as much as you do income. The profit of a business does not come from what goes out, but from what comes in.

So focus on selling, servicing and smiling … all the way to the bank.

Frankism #10

"How good you used to be doesn't matter. It's how good you're going to be that counts."

The human mind can absorb so much information that it has been described as a sponge. It soaks in everything with which it comes in contact. We take in so much information, but never let it out so it doesn't do us much good. Scientists tell us that we use very little of the capacity of our brain cells. We use so little of what God has given us.

Name any professional athlete, like a Michael Jordan (who excelled at the University of North Carolina). How good was he in high school? If he was in college and playing extremely well at the time, Uncle Frank 'sez' 'why would he care to tell you how good he once was in high school?' If you were a

43

professional team scout, why would he want to tell you how good he presently was in college? You could see that for yourself. What he would want you to know is how good he was going to be one day in the future.

As a result, he would go on to lead the Chicago Bulls to many National Championships, win many MVP trophies and an Olympic Gold Medal. He is known even today as one of the all-time greatest basketball players to ever play the game.

See, a person who is good at anything should want to be better, not any worse for goodness sakes, and surely not stay the same. It is never enough for them to be mediocre or just good at what they do. They want to excel, to achieve, to conquer and to live up to their fullest potential.

"All people who are 'great' were once 'good.' All people who are 'best' in their field were once 'one' of the best - but with hard work and dedication, they became THE best. That is something few people can say of themselves. Those who can – wouldn't. Success is a great virtue, but humility is an even greater one." - Beth Chapman

Frankism #11

"Prepare well or things you hope won't happen will occur with greater frequency than the things you hope will happen."

Many years ago Uncle Frank taught me a lesson about something called a self-fulfilling prophecy. It means that whatever we think or say for long enough will eventually happen.

Based on his intelligence and common sense, he taught me that it takes the same amount of energy to think good, positive thoughts as it does to think bad, negative thoughts. So why in the world would you not choose the first?

If you think you can succeed and you tell yourself you

45

can succeed, then it only stands to reason that you will be dedicated and work harder to succeed – thus making that dream a reality.

Uncle Frank 'sez' this is not any of that *New Age* stuff that people preach today, where you can sit on the floor and meditate for a couple of hours and make yourself a success. He said it's more like the childhood story of *The Little Engine that Could.*

You have to do more than believe in yourself and think you can do something – *you have to do it!* You have to believe in yourself, but you can't just sit on your derrière and think you can succeed – you have to put action, determination and hard work into your dreams to make them become a reality. Otherwise, they are just thoughts and lots of people have thoughts, but only those who work hard and add action to those thoughts ever fulfill their dreams.

Uncle Frank 'sez', "Big dreams combined with a little sweat equity go a long way."

Frankism #12

"It's easier to sell something – anything – if you are *interesting*. The best way to be interesting is to be *interested*."

When you meet a total stranger who comes in to do business with you they are nervous. They want to feel at ease and they want their shopping experience to be successful, enjoyable and productive. You already have something they want or they wouldn't be there. Uncle Frank says it is your job to help them find it. There is a natural tendency for people to be skeptical of salespeople, so gently help them dispel all the myths and stereotypes about us salespeople and help them meet all their shopping needs.

In order to sell a customer anything, you have to get their

attention – and the best way to get their attention is by being an interesting person. Who would want to spend time with a person who isn't interested? No one.

So how do you become interesting one might ask? You become interesting by being interested - in the other person, the customer. Their buying an item of any kind, whether it's a car or a pair of pants, is about them – all about them and never about you other than the fact that you need to be interesting. The only way you can do that is to take the focus off of yourself and put it on the other person. You are truly only as interesting as you allow them to be. Get to know them, not just because you want to sell them something, but because you genuinely care about people.

When you are self-centered, you are off-centered. Be customer-centered and you will be successful at sales and make a new friend or two along the way. That will be a double pleasure and will make you much more interested in being interesting by being interested. It is a good motivator for a salesman's or business owner's actions and reactions from his customers.

Frankism #13

"To be successful, find others that are successful and emulate them - then repeat."

C harles Caleb Cotton once said, "Imitation is the highest form of flattery." Uncle Frank 'sez' you should find someone who does what you want to do, observe how they do it best, and then repeat it. You don't have to do exactly what they do, but do it like they do.

Mr. Ray Croc decided he wanted to provide fast food restaurants with drive-through windows to serve hamburgers and fries. Someone else saw what he had done and created a similar restaurant, ...then it was Burger King, then Hardees, Wendy's, Sonic, What-a-Burger, Red Robin, and you get the point. A lot of people observed what the originators of their restaurants were doing and created others with the same basic premise. Guess what? They all sold burgers and fries through a drive-through window, and they all made money doing it.

There are many businesses to which this example applies. As a matter of fact, there are few where it doesn't apply. Someone somewhere took a successful business plan and recreated it to make it uniquely their own and became successful.

It is always good if you can find a successful business model, make a few tweaks here and there, then duplicate its success.

There are many successful people to emulate and many entrepreneurial ideas to be developed. If there is one specific field that is of interest to you, seek out a mentor in that area who will allow you to shadow them, and see for yourself what their secrets to success have been, and then reproduce them in your own unique way to fit your needs and your market's niche.

Frankism #14

"The hardest part of any task is getting started."

On your mark, get set, start! Those simple words that we have heard all of our lives still ring true today. There is preparation by being on your mark and planning ahead by getting set, but the action kicks in when the race is started.

For many people, just getting started is hard to do; but no one ever accomplished a goal, invented a product, sold a car or built a building, that didn't have to start somewhere. Uncle Frank 'sez' that there is no profession, skill or trade – as a matter of fact 'nothing that doesn't start somewhere.' There are many things that never end, but they all got started.

Starting to grow your business, creating a long-term strategic plan or a marketing plan has to begin for you to succeed. Some businesses start with $10,000 and sell only three items, others start with more or less and sell multiple, and maybe even hundreds of items, but they all started somewhere.

Uncle Frank 'sez' that sitting on your duff never got anybody anywhere in life except sitting on their duff. That's not an option if you are going to succeed. You can have the greatest ideas in the world and the grandest written business plan on earth, but if you don't get started on it, you will fail.

Every day we choose to get up and get started. The day may not go the way we want it to, but we had to get started to find out. The next day, we'll get up and get started and the day will be great, but we would have never known that either, unless we had gotten started.

Someone once said to read the obituaries each and every day. If you're not in them, then get up and get going.

Zig Ziglar says, "Read the newspaper and the Bible every day. That way you'll know what both sides are doing."

What ever your plans are – on your mark, get set (or get started), and …

GO!!!

Frankism #15

"Profit is only a dirty word if you are not providing the value necessary to dictate one."

Timing is everything, so here is a present day perfect case scenario for this famous Uncle Frank quote.

Customers don't complain about the profits that

Starbuck's or McDonald's make. However, they do complain about the profit that BP is making because their oil spill has now outweighed the value of what they are providing their customers. When that happens, the word "profit" becomes tainted and tarnished – a dirty word.

When profits are up everyone wants to talk about them. When profits are down, nobody wants to talk about them. I can understand why.

So what is a business man or business woman to do? Create a profit. Make it happen. The only time that people don't want to talk about profits is when they don't have one. The question should be why don't you have one? What are you doing right and what are you doing wrong? What can you do better? What is your competition doing better than you are? Can we find a niche or a new market?

Uncle Frank 'sez', "Any business without a profit has no business being a business and if they are one, they won't be for long."

Profit doesn't have to be a dirty word or one that promotes a negative feeling. It should be one that challenges us to take the extra steps necessary to ensure that we are working hard, providing great products and services, and whatever else is legally, morally and ethically right to turn 'profit' into a good word. It should be a word we want to talk about – because we have one.

Frankism #16

"Executing a bad idea is better than a great idea left alone."

Have you ever known someone who constantly said, 'I almost invested in that one time?', or ... 'My wife and I almost bought one of those years ago.' or ... 'My mom and I had this great idea but we just never got it off the ground.'

When Bill Gates was working on something called Microsoft many people thought he was crazy. When Henry Ford was trying to make a car on four wheels that ran on gasoline, people thought he was mad. When Einstein came up with his theory of relativity people thought he was just a freak. Uncle Frank 'sez' when they saw that wild hair of his (Einstein's), they knew he was a freak. Mr. Planters, well he was just "nuts."

55

Many great inventors, managers, creators and business people have executed bad ideas, but worked hard to develop and expand them and they became earth-shattering, award-winning ideas. They made millions and changed the course of history.

Who would have ever thought a Chia Pet would sell? I guess the couple of million people who've bought them.

All the while, I am sure that many more good ideas have died than bad ideas have made it. People can have good ideas all day long, but if they don't put action behind them it's useless energy and effort wasted.

What if Edison had not further investigated the light bulb, or Alexander Graham Bell the telephone?

Business ideas are like shoes. They look great, they are needed and useful. However, if no one ever puts feet in them, they will go nowhere.

Frankism #17

"In the sales profession, the word 'no' is just a detour sign, not a dead end."

You are traveling down the highway at 70 miles an hour with your family on your way to Disneyworld. You have been traveling all day, had to stop for gas twice and once to change a flat tire, but that was only after the State Trooper stopped you for speeding. O.K, so you weren't just going 70 mph. You just thought you were.

A couple of exits down the road you notice traffic is stopped and a sign that says 'Detour'. You realize then that you can still get where you are going if you follow the detour sign. It will just be a different route than you originally planned to take, but you take it and eventually you get there.

Had the same situation happened and the sign read 'Dead End', you would have been stopped with no way to go anywhere – just stuck there. But because there was a detour sign, you got to keep moving and arrive at the same destination, though you had to get there a different way.

In sales and in business, when someone tells you 'No', don't see it as a dead end sign, just look at it as a detour.

It may not be the right time for them to spend money or they may not be ready to buy, but eventually you know they will need to buy. Hopefully you have let them know that you have created a detour sign for them, and when they take it and come to the end, you will be there waiting to help them find the product or service they need.

If you plan to implement your plan using the right road map, there won't be any dead ends, just detours – but you will end up where you are supposed to be.

Frankism #18

"When a customer has a problem, don't shift the blame, accept responsibility."

If I've heard Uncle Frank say it once, I have heard him say it a thousand times. People don't take responsibility for what they do anymore. There are few moral absolutes in life, and people have no idea of the consequences of their actions.

Too many people and businesses have misplaced blame. They want to pass the customer with a problem around the office to six different departments, if they even return their call. The customer gets hassled, put on eternal telephone hold, and never has their concerns addressed. These are just a few of the things that drive Uncle Frank crazy.

He grew up in "the customer is always right" era, and says they still are. Well, OK, they may not always be right, but you have to keep them happy or they won't keep you in business. Uncle Frank says to always listen to the customer and that alone will satisfy them to a vast extent. Sometimes they only want to be heard. But if there is anything that you or your staff members might have done wrong, it is absolutely your responsibility to make it right.

Accept responsibility for what you and your staff do, and do everything you can to keep your customers happy and coming back time and time again. *"Go the extra mile and your customers will always leave with a smile"* is a closing thought that Uncle Frank always 'sez'.

Frankism #19

"To grow your business – don't ask what's right ... ask what's not."

B usiness is just like life – it's great when it's good and not so great when it isn't. It's easy to be on Cloud Nine and feel like a million dollars when you're making a million dollars. So what about when you're 'in the hole' a million? Not so fun, right?

Knowing what your business does right is imperative to its success. It's easy to look at, analyze and predict. It's even enjoyable to take an inventory of what your business is doing correctly.

But the true test of your desire to make your business thrive is if you are willing to find out what's wrong with it. Is your product the best that it can be? Do you have a good stock on hand? Why is your product in or not in demand? What sales incentives can you offer? How do you get new customers in the door?

You can only make something right if you know that it is wrong.

Frankism #20

"Put your ego aside and build your company with folks more talented than you, and they will push you to the top."

A person can only be so much and do so much alone. They can only know so much – alone.

The old saying of "two heads are better than one," is true. So imagine if there are ten or twenty heads more than one. That would be an intellectual gold mine.

A person can be as smart as ever and if they don't surround themselves with good people, they will not ever rise to the excellence of their potential.

Uncle Frank had a friend that used to play tennis. This friend always sought out lesser players than he was so he could win and he did. Uncle Frank told him if he ever wanted to get any better, that he needed to only play people who were better than he was, so the level of his game could improve.

The man went from being a "B" player to being an "A" player after he got beat over and over again by someone who was better than he was. It challenged him and while he was a good player, playing with a better person made him a great player.

You are only as good as the people you surround yourself with in your business and in your life. Challenge yourself, and don't be intimidated by hiring someone better or smarter than you are, because they will challenge you and help you to become the best that you can be.

Egos can become a huge hindrance to success. A person can drown in themselves if they're not careful. Staying "grounded" is important.

Uncle Frank 'sez', *"Keep your ego in check and check it at the door when you go into work, are two tidbits of good advice."*

He also 'sez' it's easy to put this into perspective, and that we all learned it when we were children, but just don't forget the lesson that still holds true today: *"Don't get too big for your britches."*

Frankism #21

"Sending three thank you notes a day will keep customers coming your way."

A sales letter or advertisement is no good without a follow up or a personal touch. Sending a thank you note is imperative to building relationships and having a high rate of return from your customers. If you respect them, appreciate them and thank them with sincerity, they'll be your customers for life. They'll also become your friends for life.

65

When you "sell" them – thank them. If you send three thank you notes a day you will impress your customers and business associates. If you send three hand-written thank you notes a day, you will blow their minds.

Writing thank you notes today is a lost art. Few people write anything, much less a hand-written note – especially to thank a customer for their business.

In a troubled economy you need more than ever to show gratitude and appreciation to the people who put bread on your table.

Be sure to always thank anybody who shows you an act of kindness — and doing business with you is definitely an act of kindness.

Frankism #22

"If there is not a customer 'experience' at your business, they will seek one elsewhere."

Uncle Frank was named after his grandpa, who started the first Frank Myers store eighty-three years ago. Uncle Frank remembers with great fondness a story that Grandpa Myers told him about two men who owned little country stores just across the road from each other in his community.

One man was a Mr. Roy Black and one was Mr. B. They both sold ice cream. They both charged the same amount for their ice cream. Their stores looked about the same in appearance. They were both good people. But there were always twice as many people at Roy Black's store than Mr. B's store. Why, you might ask?

Grandpa Frank said when you went into Mr. B's store he would say, "Hello, what can I get for you?" When you told him "ice cream," he proceeded to get it for you, hand it to you, tell you how much it cost, take your money, say "thank you", and off you went.

When you went into Roy Black's store he said, "Hey, how are you today? How is your family? Isn't it a beautiful day? How can I help you?"

You would tell him you wanted ice cream, and he would tell you all the different flavors he had and ask you if you wanted to sample one. Then he would proceed to make you an ice cream cone and offer you a chair to sit down while you stayed a little while, ate your ice cream, and talked with him. If you had children with you, he would even sit them in his lap while they ate theirs and he talked with you.

When you were ready to leave, he would thank you, get up from his chair, and walk you to the door to say 'goodbye'. When you got in the car he would wave goodbye to you and say, "Come back to see me," and you would, of course. Who wouldn't when they were treated so cordially?

Mr. B offered you ice cream but Roy Black offered you ice cream and an "experience." It was an experience that Grandpa Frank remembered all of his life and passed on to Uncle Frank, who continues to pass it to the next generation in our family.

I am fortunate to have learned the life lesson and simple business model of Roy Black. It has helped me in training my staff on the true method of how to treat a customer to keep them coming back for more.

Frankism #23

"If you have to lie to sell something, you are not a salesperson, you are a liar!"

Good salespeople know how to "win friends and influence people." It's not just the name of a former number one best-selling book. It is what good salespeople do best.

Selling is an art, a skill and a gift. It is a profession and a noble one when done correctly and in an honest way, which is the only way to do it. When selling, there may be some bartering or negotiating at the table, but it will never be done under the table.

A 'sell' to a salesman is just like a field goal to a kicker – it is what they are trained to do and what they do best. It is an honest living, but not just something they are paid to do.

You can lie about the size of fish that you catch, but only if you take it back and say you were just joking. But you can never, ever lie about anything, and especially not anything that has to do with something you have to sell. It's really not worth the credibility you will lose and the customers you will lose too.

A salesman by any other name is still a salesman, and a liar by any other name is still - well, just a liar ...and will always be a liar. Nothing good ever comes from being a liar. Uncle Frank 'sez', *"You may not like what I say, but it will always be the truth!"*

Because of that statement, you never have to worry about anything Uncle Frank tells you. You always know where he is on any issue.

Frankism #24

"Avoiding an argument is the best way to win one."

Benjamin Franklin said, "An ounce of prevention is worth a pound of cure." Well, Uncle Frank 'sez', "The best way to win an argument is to avoid one." That's preventive medicine at its best.

Uncle Frank is a smart man. He doesn't get in many arguments – only the ones that have to do with legal, religious, moral or ethical standards. He'll stand up for those things in a New York minute. But overall, he tries to avoid arguments. That's one of the many reasons Uncle Frank is such a well-respected man in his community.

However, let there be no mistake that when he does get into an argument, he is right. If you don't think so just ask him,

73

and he will tell you.

There is a certain point in a conversation where everything that can be said has been said. A smart man knows to move on, walk away and "let sleeping dogs lie," as they say. But an even smarter man knows not to argue in the first place.

As God's creatures, we are given the ability to have and use common sense if we choose to do so. If we do, we know that it is much better to state our case, give our opinion, hear the other person's, and if we disagree, then agree to disagree. It's just that simple.

There is no reason to get into an argument when you can avoid one altogether. If you do, your relationships will last longer and you will respect yourself, but not nearly as much as the other guy or gal will. *Uncle Frank believes we should live by example and we all know that Uncle Frank practices what he preaches.*

Avoid arguments when you can and you'll win every time.

Uncle Frank 'sez', *"If you don't have an argument, you don't have to worry about who wins and who loses, because everyone wins."*

Frankism #25

"The customer isn't always right, but they're never wrong."

Years ago there was a motto that claimed, "The customer is always right." It's a self-explanatory statement and to a great extent it is still true.

If the customer doesn't like the way their steak was cooked, you don't argue with them about how they said they wanted it cooked, you don't explain the cooking process your kitchen staff uses, or that your regular chef is out because his wife's mother died of cancer and was buried in Alaska, so he had to take a week off to go to Alaska for the funeral, etc., etc.

What you do is apologize to the customer, confirm how they want it cooked, take it to the kitchen have it cooked that way and ensure that it is before you deliver it to the customer to confirm that it is correct this time just before you apologize again. If they are still not happy with it, you offer them a refund and apologize to them yes, again.

Times have changed quite a bit in that there are people who go out to intentionally scam businesses. They may drop a hair in their food to get it free, or give you the old dine-and-dash routine. They may switch price tags on clothing in an effort to get it cheaper or any number of things.

People who are dishonest will find a way to be dishonest and you have to learn to spot them. However, you can still treat them with kindness. OK, so you have to be stern with them and let them know that you can't be taken advantage of, and sometimes it's just best to give them what they want, and quietly and politely ask them to consider doing business elsewhere in the future.

The bottom line is that the customer that you want and need to keep is always right. Also remember to look at every single person as a potential customer and one that you want to keep. Otherwise, you won't have very many.

So Uncle Frank is right as usual, the customer is always right unless they're wrong and even then for the most part, you have to treat them like they're right. It's just the right thing to do.

Frankism #26

"A little bit of kindness will go a long way, but a lot of kindness will go a whole lot farther."

Another valuable lesson I learned from Uncle Frank is to always be kind to people.

Business accessories, new computers to expedite the processes of your business, buying new office furniture and hiring more employees are all good for attracting customers to your business. They are all important factors and they all cost money.

But kindness is a virtue, and treating your clients or customers with kindness is a necessity, if you plan on staying in business for very long.

While all those other items are investments in your business and cost you money, kindness doesn't cost you one single penny. Being kind and expecting your employees to be kind is easy, and costs you not one thin dime. But the return on that investment is perhaps one of the greatest in your business.

The return you get from your investment of kindness is excellent "word-of-mouth" publicity – worth ten times a typical newspaper, radio or television advertisement.

Another return you get is more customers, repeat customers and new customers. That's an enormous return on an investment that costs nothing.

Go the extra mile to smile, be nice, friendly, courteous and genuinely kind to people and it will come back to you and your business ten times over – again and again and again. That's what Uncle Frank 'sez'.

Frankism #27

"The Golden Rule is not just a rule; it is a business principle worth keeping."

As children we all learned the Golden Rule in school. "Do unto others as you would have them do unto you."

It is more than a lesson or a "rule." It is a moral value and a business principle too.

Don't try to sell anyone on anything you wouldn't buy for yourself. Don't charge them any price that is so outrageous you wouldn't be willing to pay it yourself for the same product.

Uncle Frank tells a story about a man whose daughter was

marrying a builder who was down on his luck. The building business was not at its best.

The man asked his future son-in-law to build him a house and he would pay him for it. He wanted it built, painted and completed in its entirety. He asked his future son-in-law to make it the absolute nicest, best that he possibly could. He wanted top notch everything.

The builder started building the house, but because he wanted to make more money than he should have off it, he cut every corner he could possibly cut. He used the cheapest supplies and the cheapest paint, light fixtures and accessories. The foundation already had a crack in it, but the builder covered over it feeling confident that no one would ever know.

He built the deck with the cheapest wood possible and the walls of the house were as paper thin as possible.

When he completed the house he took the key to his future father-in-law and handed him the key.

The man said, "Thank you," as he handed the key back and told the builder that it was his wedding present to him and his daughter.

How do you think the builder would have built the house had he known he was building it for himself and his future bride?

He would have built it the total opposite of what he did. Now he would have to live in it.

"Do unto others as you would have them do unto you."

Remember and follow ...*The Golden Rule*.

Always!

Frankism #28

"Be organized and you'll be prepared for anything."

Sir Winston Churchill once said, "To every man there comes in his lifetime that special moment when he is figuratively tapped on the shoulder and offered a chance to do a very special thing, unique to him and fitted to his talents, what a tragedy if that moment finds him unprepared or unqualified for that which would be his finest hour."

Wouldn't it be a shame if the moment came for you to be tapped on the shoulder and you weren't prepared? If you had the opportunity of a lifetime, but had to give it up because you didn't have the bills paid, the new employee hired, the proper stock in inventory or your office air conditioning system repaired.

Find me an organized person, and I'll find you a person who can be tapped on the shoulder at any given time and who is ready to take on the world.

Being organized is the one thing that can save you hours and hours of valuable time. One hour spent organizing your desk and office can save you three hours looking for something you need.

People always fear audits, but not the organized person. They welcome them, and if the IRS audits them they may find they owe their business money - instead of the other way around.

A good business investment is to be totally organized in all of your offices and departments. Make sure you have good records, but they will do you no good if they are not properly organized.

The organization of all that you have in stock is important too. Inventories are really not big bears for the people who have everything in order.

So when your time comes to be tapped on the shoulder to expand your business horizons, you'll be ready.

Frankism #29

"Never say never when you can say whenever, wherever and however."

Uncle Frank has never had the word "never" in his vocabulary. He has taught me that simple business principle. The only time that it is acceptable to say never is when someone asks you if you are going to give up. Otherwise, never say never – never.

Believing you can do something is 90% of doing it. If you don't believe in yourself, no one else will, according to Uncle Frank.

Being confident in yourself is not something you just do. You'd better train yourself to do what you do and continue to learn long after the class or training session is over.

Sales and life are the same – in that we need continuing education in them both. That may or may not mean formal classes, but observation and learning from your associates and peers as well as your mistakes.

Uncle Frank 'sez' mistakes are alright as long as you don't continue to repeat the same ones over and over again. You just need to consider them as lessons along the way.

Frankism #30

"Don't say anything you wouldn't say if you had to repeat it."

If you want to earn the respect of other people, make sure never to say anything behind their backs that you wouldn't say to their face. Say nothing that you would be embarrassed to repeat.

Uncle Frank lives by this rule – to the point that if you don't want to know what he thinks, then you shouldn't ask him. If you do, he will quickly tell you.

That's just one of a thousand things that set him apart from hundreds of other businessmen I've known. You never, ever have to wonder where Uncle Frank stands on any subject or issue. All you had to do was ask. Why do you think the name of this book is *Uncle Frank 'sez?'*

While some people may not like that kind of raw honesty, I do. You don't have to guess what they're thinking or wanting to say, but won't.

They are honest with you and it saves an awful lot of time, energy and effort playing the guessing game.

That way you can get down to business and get the job at hand done.

Frankism #31

"Being flexible will help you bend, but never break."

The ability to be flexible is a prerequisite in the business world. Sometimes things just happen and they have to be taken care of at that exact moment.

Sometimes we have family emergencies or doctor's appointments, or goodness forbid, a funeral to attend.

As business people we have to take care of business, but we

also have to take care of our families and ourselves too.

We must work hard, be prepared for anything, and flexible in order to accommodate the things that we can't prepare for sometimes.

Many people will work themselves to death, not take care of themselves, and just about have a complete nervous breakdown.

Uncle Frank is a big believer in living a balanced life and setting your priorities accordingly.

A good business person knows how to bend and bend and bend without ever breaking. They know when to stop, when to seek help, and when to take a break to keep from breaking.

If you want to live to see your business grow, take care of yourself so you can take care of your business.

Uncle Frank 'sez', *"Work hard – play hard – pray hard!"*

Frankism #32

"Always practice the 3 F's with people: fair, firm and friendly."

Uncle Frank has always been fair and friendly, but he can be quite firm too.

He is firm with people because he wants so badly to challenge them to do their best and to challenge themselves to succeed.

He has always been hardest on us – his family – because he loves us and expects more out of us. He pushes us to reach our fullest potential, not for his sake, but for ours. He wants us to succeed, to be self-sufficient and happy.

It's easy to be friendly, a little more challenging at times to be fair. But it is oftentimes more difficult than not to be firm with people, especially those we love.

Thank goodness Uncle Frank taught me how to live by the 3 F's. It has really helped me in dealing with my family, friends and employees too. Friendly, fair and firm when need be, makes good relationships with mutual respect and understanding.

"Fair, firm and friendly…"

Frankism #33

"Strive to be your best and you will be."

There is a line in the movie *Talladega Nights* where a former race car driver tells his son who also was a race car driver, "If you ain't first – you're last." Uncle Frank might have well come up with that quote if Will Ferrell hadn't come up with it first.

You need to always strive to be the best at what you do. As the old U.S. Army slogan says, "Be all that you can be." What a great challenge! Few of us ever live up to our fullest potential. Just imagine what we could accomplish if we did.

You have to believe that you can be the best at what you do, or you never will be. If you don't believe it, then who else will? Strive to be the best that you can be, set that example for those who work around you and hopefully they will follow suit.

If a competitor is doing something better than you are, then figure out how to do it not just better, but the best that it can be done. Don't let anyone else outsmart you.

Remember, "If you ain't first, you're last." Well, not really, but as Uncle Frank would say, "Don't play second fiddle to nobody." Play first fiddle, be the best fiddler and play as long and as hard as you can, so you can stay there. Do what you do best and you will.

"If you aren't first, you really aren't last, but you aren't first either."

Frankism #34

"Time is more than just money – it's time, and time is more important to some people than money these days."

There is no customer in the world that wants to wait in a long line for anything. We live in a fast-paced, hectic society where everyone wants instant results. Whatever it is that your customer wants, rest assured they wanted it yesterday, so today is far too late. Get them what they want, get it quickly and easily and they'll love you forever. Just be sure not to let the speed of light at which they want it interfere with the quality of it.

People may want your product, but they want fast, convenient ways to pay for it and be "processed" through your system.

The last thing customers want is to be inconvenienced. They don't want any red tape that holds them up, and, depending on what you are selling, they don't want to have to tote it to their car either. They want quick delivery on one hand, and quick, exceptional service – whether you have a new computer system or not – on the other.

Customers want a great product with good service, and the opportunity to purchase or not purchase additional items to accompany it. What they want most is to get all of the above and to get it now.

Another thing that Uncle Frank has noticed are those stores where you go to spend hundreds, sometimes thousands of dollars a year. When you have purchased your items that you have already paid for and are walking out the door, someone demands to see your itemized receipt. He thinks that's rude and it is.

One day an elderly man who thought he was a middle linebacker for the Chicago Bears tried to chase poor old Uncle Frank down in the parking lot to see his receipt. Uncle Frank was offended and told the man so. After all, Uncle Frank wouldn't even dream of stealing anything, and he didn't fit the profile of someone who would steal anything either.

Just treat your customers with the same kindness and courtesy you would expect a business to treat you with, and you'll all be just fine. In everything you do put your customer and their wants and needs ahead of your own, and you'll be successful.

Uncle Frank 'sez' to tell you that whatever you do, don't tackle them at the exit door just because you can't see their receipt. Always treat them with respect.

"Customers want a great product with good service

...what they want most is to get it all...now."

Frankism #35

"Know Your Product and Your Process or Find a New Job."

You know what Uncle Frank 'sez' to people that don't want to learn his tried and true customer friendly processes? "Don't let the door hit you where the good Lord split you."

Knowing how to sell the sizzle, build value in the package and creatively deliver a product is as important as the product itself. Employees need to learn how important it is to be consistent with their company's processes.

Most department stores offer gift wrapping in beautiful boxes to their customers. In fact, it's become so common that most people take the added value for granted. However, if that same gift is wrapped in a beautiful box with a red ribbon and the famous Neiman-Marcus gold sticker, then the value of that gift increases. The gift wrap itself is not as important as the *way* the gift wrap was packaged and presented.

Not only do you need to be *the* expert on your product, but your process as well. If you're not, your competitor will be. You need to know how to prepare, present and deliver your product in a way that makes it an extraordinary experience for your customer. Remember that **YOU** are the authority and the expert on every aspect of your product and **YOU** must create a process that makes them say "WOW!"

You have to know why your product is better than everybody else's and be prepared to prove it. Uncle Frank 'sez' that we're living in a "show me" world and lip service just won't do it anymore. Be prepared to give a world class product demonstration because it is a necessity in today's market place (and the more testimonials you can provide from extremely satisfied customers never hurt either).

Uncle Frank 'sez' you also need to know your processes just as well. Know the correct way to greet a customer and treat them like a guest in your home. A big warm smile and going the extra mile will always pay off for you in the long run.

Don't be afraid or embarrassed to tout your product's reliability, dependability, affordability and money-back guarantee. No customer wants a salesperson who doesn't use and love their own product. Besides, if it's the best there is, then why wouldn't you?

Take pride in what you do and know how to do it efficiently, effectively and better than anyone else.

Frankism #36

"Lack of Integrity is NOT the problem. The problem is that we can't see how badly we lack it."

It's easy to get caught up in life, in the heat of the moment or the excitement of a good business deal. It's equally as easy to relax our honesty and integrity a little too, if we're not totally grounded. We should never let our integrity slide or our moral values relax even a little.

It's far easier to talk about integrity than to have it and to show it in every single situation in our lives.

According to the dictionary, integrity means, "Steadfast adherence to a strict ethical or moral code."

In order to adhere to something, we must know what it

103

means. We must understand it before we can adhere to it.

Adherence to integrity doesn't just mean when things go well, but when they don't as well.

When a client is bartering with us, or when one has no earthly idea of what the mark up on an item is, we need to always act and react with integrity in mind.

Just like with anything else – practice makes perfect, *so make integrity a part of whom and what you are, no matter where you are or what you are doing.*

Frankism #37

"The standards set for you by others can't be higher than the ones you set for yourself."

You are responsible for you. You are the best you and the only you, that you will ever have. Don't let other people have to set standards for you. They may not set them high enough or they may set them too high. You know where they need to be, and you are the one that will have to achieve and accomplish them – so you set them for yourself.

No one knows your capabilities, talents, skills and abilities better than you do. Only you know what you have within your spirit and what you can do – *so set your goals and go for them!*

We should live lives in which we want to set our goals and standards, based on what we have to offer the world and on what we have to give. We should set the bar where we want and need it to be, but it should be at what we consider to be our best performance, not the safest or easiest one.

We should also have enough confidence in our abilities – to never allow anyone else to believe more in us, or to set higher standards for us, than we would for ourselves.

Frankism #38

"Don't spend your energy on making excuses. Invest in getting results."

Do you realize that it takes the same amount of time, energy and effort to make excuses as it does to correct the problem? As a matter of fact, some people would argue that it takes less time, energy and effort to resolve a problem, instead of talking about why it is the way it is, who dropped the ball on the project, etc., etc.

Far too many people want to complain about things. One of those things they love to complain about is our government. They talk about all the things that are wrong with it, never realizing that at least we have one – whereas many people across the globe don't.

What's worse is that these same people will complain for

hours about all that is wrong with the government. While I agree that there are issues with it, I would be remiss not to point out that there is much good about it too.

One of those really good things is that we can participate in our government if we choose to do so.

The whiners and complainers, when asked, will oftentimes tell you that they do not vote.

Uncle Frank 'sez', *"If you don't vote, then you have no right to complain."* There is a great deal of truth to that.

If everyone who complained about government would cast their votes and let their voices be heard at their polling place, they could change our government as they see fit.

This would take the same amount of energy and effort, if not less, than to constantly complain about it.

Frankism #39

"It's easier to maintain your integrity than try to recover it."

Words and actions, once released or completed, cannot be taken back. It is like the oxygen you breathe out of your lungs – once you release it, it is gone! You may be able to take in other oxygen, but that particular amount is gone forever. You cannot get it back.

That is why watching what we say and do is so vitally important. It speaks volumes about who and what we are. It tells other people what type of values and principles we do or do not possess.

It is so much easier to maintain our values and principles than to recover or retrieve them. Once a person loses their good name or their reputation, it is hard to restore it – if they can even get it back at all.

Some people make mistakes that take years to recover from – bankruptcy is one good example. Once it is on your record, it is very difficult to get it removed. It affects you for years to come, as financiers don't want to do business with you or loan you money – because of the risk they consider you to be, based on your financial history.

Uncle Frank has always encouraged me to consider the importance of integrity in my personal and professional life. He says it is something you should have and hold onto – otherwise, it will be very difficult to recover and could be lost forever.

Frankism #40

"We are all blessed with the power of choice, so choose wisely."

God blessed us (or cursed us) with the power to make our own choices – it just depends on how we use those choices as to which way we look at his gift to us.

It is nice of our Creator to allow us to choose – until, that is, we make the wrong choices. If you've lived even five minutes on this earth, then you are bound to have made a few wrong choices.

The one thing that all people have in common is the right and the ability to make their own choices.

Let's look at some of the people in history who had choices and how they used them: Mother Teresa had choices, but so did Hitler. Adam and Eve had a choice, but so did the disciples. Osama Bin Laden sadly had a choice to make, and so do the troops who fight against him and his regime.

It's not the choices that get us in trouble – it's what we do with them that can either make or break us.

Everyone has choices: choices to do good or bad, to be positive or negative, to be your very best or to just get by. *Which choices will you make in your life?*

Frankism #41

"You can sell the sizzle all you want, but if the steak 'tastes like crap' - no one is gonna order it again!"

Uncle Frank 'sez' you can create excitement, blow up balloons, have fancy advertising with bright colored flashing lights and the whole ball of wax, but if your product and your service aren't any good, then none of it matters.

All the tricky gimmicks in the world that some businesses use won't get them good customers. In turn, all the positive, good things that you can do won't let you keep your customers unless you make good on your offers and keep your word.

You can't just tell them you are going to give them a good deal, that you will work with them to meet their price, that you will give them top quality service at affordable prices to go along with their warranty, ...**YOU HAVE TO DELIVER!**

You have to make the sizzle pop AND cook the steak the way they want it – to keep 'em coming back for more.

Frankism #42

"Energize your vision through faith and give it momentum through hard work."

It's one thing to think about vision and to write a vision statement for your business or your life. But your vision has to have feet to move. It has to be energized through faith in yourself and faith in God. Uncle Frank says that prayer and faith will add wings to your vision and make you soar.

Helen Keller, both deaf and blind, once said of vision, "The only thing worse than being blind is having sight but no *vision*."

In addition to energizing your vision, you must give it momentum to grow and endure through hard work. Your

115

vision must last through the good times and the bad, and you must stay focused on it no matter what gets in the way.

CONCLUSION

By now, you have learned enough about what Uncle Frank 'sez', so that you should be feeling smarter and smarter by the minute.

There are many life lessons in the quotes and stories of Uncle Frank that can greatly enhance your vision and improve the quality of your life.

Uncle Frank 'sez' it's all in this book, just read it and discover it for yourself. He also 'sez', "Life is what you make it, so get up and do the best you can with what you've got, and you'll be the best you can be with what you have."

It is my hope that through reading this book you have gained insight into how to live life a little better and a whole lot smarter. It is my hope, and Uncle Frank's too, that you become more and more successful in your life's every endeavor, both personally and professionally.

These are words of wisdom and wit – advice from a man who has written the book on valuable life lessons. So when you come up against a rough spot on the road of life, or you're hanging at the end of your rope, searching for some good business advice, or a word of encouragement and support - just remember all that you've read. Remember all that Uncle Frank 'sez', and you and your life will be all the better for it.

And so, in his parting shot, Uncle Frank 'Sez":

"Failing doesn't make you a failure. Quitting does...
NEVER QUIT!"

ABOUT TRACY

Tracy Myers is a car dealership owner, author, speaker and entrepreneur. He recently celebrated the opening of his newest business, The Celebrity Academy in Charlotte, NC. The Academy teaches professionals, entrepreneurs and business owners how to get noticed, gain instant credibility, make millions and dominate their competition by building their celebrity expert status.

Following these principles have helped Tracy gain enormous success at his own dealership, Frank Myers Auto Maxx. It was recently recognized as the Number One Small Businesses in NC by Business Leader Magazine, one of the top three dealerships to work for in the country by The Dealer Business Journal, and one of the Top 22 Independent Automotive Retailers in the United States by Auto Dealer Monthly Magazine.

Tracy Myers graduated from the Certified Master Dealer program at Northwood University and was the youngest person to receive the National Quality Dealer Of The Year award, which is the highest obtainable honor in the used car industry.

He has provided guest commentary on the FOX Business Network and has also been featured on NBC, ABC, CBS & FOX affiliates across the country. He has appeared on stages from North Carolina to San Francisco and is the author of several books, including: *Car Buying Secrets Exposed: The Dirty Little Secrets of a Used Car Dealer* and *YOU Are The Brand, Stupid!*

Tracy and his wife Lorna have made their home in Lewisville, NC with their 2 children Maddie and Presley. He is a self-proclaimed Christian Business Owner whose goal is to run his business "By the Book".

Read more about Tracy at www.TracyMyers.com

www.ingramcontent.com/pod-product-compliance
Lightning Source LLC
Chambersburg PA
CBHW020449100426
42813CB00031B/3310/J